1001 Places To Pee
Before You Die

Catty Comments and Praise for Benson's Stories

"My first-graders love Benson's letters. You would have thought that I had just given them their favorite thing for Christmas.... Yes, they were that excited! They are still amazed that he can write so much! They were glued to the words, following me every step of the way, and laughing on cue. It was priceless! I do know that you already have eighteen little fans with my class. They can't wait for the next adventure."

Debbie Johnson
First-grade teacher
Ledgemont Elementary School, Thompson, Ohio

"What Benson says isn't true. One day shelties *will* rule the world!"

Chauncy
Ruler of the Shelties,
From Germany to Virginia

"Benson, why would I recommend your book? I mean seriously, you're such a dog. You may be a strapping figure of a dog boy, but you stare at me with your tongue out, and that one time—against my better judgment, I must add—I let you get way too close and you about burned my whiskers off with your breath. Dude, eat a fish mint or something! If you really want to impress me or any self-absorbed cat woman, you'll have to be a bit more subtle. Your stories aren't half bad. Don't get any ideas though. It's not like we're married or anything, dog breath!"

Sophie
The Cat Queen Next Door
Springfield, Virginia

"Benson's insights into the human condition are nothing short of amazing. This book is a must-read for any savvy canine who is still training the humans in the house. Move over Stephen Covey. Benson's habits are both charming and disarming. Finally, a new bark in the self-help, tell-all genre."

Lili (Schnauzer) Doyal
Kansas City, Missouri

1001 Places to Pee Before You Die

By
Benson and Mari K. Eder

ISBN: 978-0-557-06613-1

This book is dedicated to my grandma and granddad because they made sure I had the best mama. My mama says I can be anything I want to be, including a real boy.

Contents

Acknowledgments

This book started as a simple thank-you note from me to the wonderful North Carolina couple who allowed me to adopt their rambunctious six-month-old miniature schnauzer puppy, Benson. Although they gave him up reluctantly, they also knew that he could be quite a handful, even if a terrifically loveable, mischievous, and intelligent handful. I adopted Benson in May 2004. Wayne and Janet Dishman sent him a birthday card and present in August and did the same at Christmas that year. So I composed several thank-you notes, at first from me, but later from Benson himself. After all, they wanted to hear from him most of all.

Special thanks to my great friend and editor, Paul Turk. Special thanks to Benson's editor, reader, and webmaster, Mary Pat Begin-Ortiz. I owe a great debt to Auntie Debra, who now shares snacks, recipes, and treats with Benson. Thank you to Jeff Clune and Joe Schreiber for more recipes and support. Thank you to Ruth Gulliver for the cover photo. Thank you to all of my friends and relatives who encouraged me to tell Benson's stories. Special thanks to Debbie Johnson for sharing Benson's stories with her first-grade students.

Finally, thank you to Judy McLendon for the gift of Benson.

Mari K. Eder
Springfield, Virginia

INTRODUCTION

MAMA's INTRODUCTION: I found it very easy to write in Benson's voice. He is very expressive, and it is easy to see how he thinks and looks at the world around him. It is great fun for me to try to look at life the way I think he might. At twenty-eight pounds, Benson is large for a miniature schnauzer and can be very brave, like a big dog. He can likewise be a sweet and cuddly puppy, but only if no one is looking. His presence in my life has been a true dogsend. He helps me relax after days of incredible stress and pressure, and in his own way, he knows how to entertain, to comfort, and to get me to play with him and a chew toy on the living room floor. After a twelve- to fourteen-hour day in the Pentagon, wading into Benson's world is truly refreshing.

Eventually I began sharing these letters with about thirty of my friends who are also dog lovers. I've found that many of them now share "the Benson letters," passing them along to their friends. At least once a month, someone new writes to tell me how much they enjoy these letters.

Benson's stories are usually a little bit funny, sometimes uplifting, and most of them have a little life lesson in them as well—about courtesy, telling the truth, being nice to neighbors, earning an allowance, etc. I don't think Benson will run out of things to talk about anytime soon.

BENSON'S INTRUODUCTION: My name is Benson. I'm a minia-ture schnauzer, and because my birthday is in August, I'm a Leo. I moved to Virginia in 2004 when I was six months old to live with my new mama and her sister, the chef. I call her Auntie Debra. Mama always said she would have another dog when she found one who needed a good home, so I packed up my suitcase and winter coat and ventured forth from my native North Carolina.

My grandparents in North Carolina still send me birthday and Christmas cards and letters, so last year I decided I needed to do a better job of answering and thanking them. I write them every month now, and Mama helps me. I am a very good dog boy—the best ever, if you listen to some people, and when they talk like that I do listen. So these are my letters to Grandma and Granddad. I wrote them for the first time after Christmas last year because I wanted to say thank you for the treats and toys they sent. Then I posed for pictures to send them. Mama says I am very spoiled and that I am a ham. What I know is that I'm registered (whatever that means), and my registered name is really silly. It is "Benson's Best Behavior." Mama says she named me that because she hoped I'd live up to it one day. Ha ha ha. That isn't nice.

I have a red collar with bones on it and all kinds of charms that rattle when I run. Mama calls them my bling. I like all people except bad and mean ones, and all dogs except Smokey next door. And I always tell only true things to my grandma, so you will like these stories.

CHAPTER 1

Sunday Adventures

First I want to tell you about my Sunday adventures. On Sundays I get to go for a long walk. That means I am ready to get up early on Sunday mornings, usually when it starts to get light, DPT (that's Doggie Plotting Time for those who don't know, or about 6:30 AM people time). I keep trying to get Mama to wake up so we can go. Usually I start out nice—I lick Mama's ears and nose and sigh a lot. That doesn't work very often.

Sometimes Mama will tell me to go back to sleep, and I do. But after another hour of DPT, I'm very impatient. I have found that the best way to wake Mama up is for me to get up on Mama's pillow and wrap myself around her head. Then I can lick her ears and she can't get away. After Mama is awake and upright, I jump down to the floor and bite her toes. This encourages her to get dressed quickly. Running away with her socks works too.

By now I'm pretty excited, so I bark and growl until we get downstairs and Mama gets her coat. Last Sunday it was cold, so I had to wear my green Chia Pet sweater. It does keep me warm, even if I do look like a little wuss dog in it. Off we went.

We walked down the hill in our development, all the way to the end. I know where every dog lives, so I look for them on their decks or in the windows. When I see them I look away really fast and strut. I am out for the big adventure with my mama. They aren't.

3

At the end of the road there is a path in the woods. It goes down a little hill and over a teeny stream. I have to time it just right so I can jump over the water because I hate to get my feet wet. Then we go under the big highway and beside a big creek and walk toward the neighborhood park where there are baseball fields for little kids. It is a pretty big park, and there is never anyone there on Sunday mornings, especially that early.

Last Sunday we saw some Canada geese on the ball field. They made awful honking noises and smelled bad too. I wanted to chase them, but Mama said no. She said these are the geese who forgot to migrate, so they just stay here and complain all winter. Mama says we have some relatives like that.

Then we walked over to the creek to look at the water. We don't do this often, but Mama hates trash in the woods and picks it up and puts it in one of my bags if I haven't used them. There was something swimming in the water! I thought it looked like a dog, so I sniffed hard in case I should be barking. Besides, I couldn't imagine why any dog would take a bath voluntarily. When the critter saw me, it slapped its tail on the water and dove under! The sound was real loud, and I jumped and hid behind Mama's legs. Mama looked back at me and said, "You aren't a great hunter, are you?" Well, that wasn't very nice because I didn't know we were hunting. No one told *me*. Mama explained it was a beaver and that beavers live in dams. There was an old tree there, halfway in the water, so that must be where the beaver lives.

Finally I got to run. When Mama takes off the leash, I can run and run until all of the running is done. You remember how much I liked to run as a puppy, right? Mama says the little wild dog goes down the hill, and the tired, happy dog comes back.

I find lots of good stuff to sniff on our walks too. One time I found a baseball, and another time I found a sock. I'm not allowed to keep anything though. Mama keeps trying to teach me how to fetch, but I really don't see the point. Why should I do all the work, especially for a stick, when I never get to keep anything I find?

I was tired after all the excitement with the geese and the beaver. Mama thinks that's a good thing; one of our neighbors said there are foxes in the woods too, and Mama thinks I would chase one if I saw it. I might, especially if it looks like a dog; I bet they run really fast. I can't even catch a squirrel, and I've tried really hard.

After Mama put my leash back on and we started back toward the path in the woods, I saw what looked like a very big dog. It was pretty far away, but Mama stopped and didn't move. I stopped too, even though I wanted to ask what it was. It had long tree branches on its head and smelled like the wild. Finally it walked through the creek and went up the hill into the thicket. Mama told me it was a buck. I've never seen a buck before, and it was really *big*. I know now that a buck is a kind of deer because Maddie told me.

Maddie used to be my girlfriend until she became a grown-up Labrador retriever. Now she runs with a different crowd, but we still play if we're at my house or hers. She likes to fetch, and she knows all about ducks and geese and deer. We disagree about swimming however. I bet she hasn't seen that beaver.

Grandma, the best part about my Sunday walks is that sometimes afterward I get bacon and toast. I'm usually really hungry after being out in the woods, and bacon is the best thing to have then, especially if someone makes me have a bath if mud and leaves are stuck to my beard. Then I really deserve a treat.

CHAPTER 2
KIDNAPPED BY ALIENS

I want to tell you first that I am very brave. I am not a little yappy dog, and I'm not like a big, dumb dog that picks fights. I am a brave protector! I look out the window every day and protect our home from people who dare to park their cars in the area or walk on my grass. I growl real low at people who try to get close to my mama too.

But there are a few little things that do scare me—a little.

I don't like it when things that aren't real move—all by themselves. I don't like it when trash can lids rock back and forth, and then move down the sidewalk, blown by the wind. It's just too much like a ghost did it. I don't even like it when a single leaf swirls around in circles all by itself in the middle of the street.

Mama says my ears are like the blue lights on top of a police car. They wiggle back and forth when I see something strange or a movement I don't like. She knows that I will look at anything new, out of place, or unusual. A really scary thing happened one day when one of our neighbors had a baby. They put pink balloons on the handrail by the steps to their front door. I saw that balloon moving all by itself and I wanted to *run*, but Mama said it was okay. Whew! I thought it was coming to get me.

To prove to me that it was okay, Auntie Debra bought me a balloon (with Scooby-Doo on it!) from the grocery store one day and let me play with it. That way I could tell it was nothing to be scared of—nothing at all! Now I like balloons. I don't get them as a present very often; they are a special treat. Mama says we play something called volleyball whenever I get a balloon. I bap the balloon across the living room to Mama, and she whacks it back at me. We play until it bursts. I like balloons now, and they aren't scary at all.

Mama and I had a little talk before Halloween last year, and I understand all about pumpkins now. They are okay as long as they stay still. But when there are candles in them and scary faces it looks like they are moving. Sometimes I'm afraid they will bite me.

But there is one thing still that really scares me—the smoke alarm.

Last summer the smoke alarm went off in the hallway downstairs. Mama said later the battery was going dead, and when that happens, it beeps every two or three minutes. I didn't like that sound *at all*. It sounded like aliens from outer space were coming to kidnap me. It was really high pitched and squawky, like the aliens were talking. I ran into the basement and hid. By the time Mama got home from work, I was scared to death. I was hiding by the back door and shaking real hard and drooling. I don't know why. I think I forgot my mouth was open.

Mama thought I was sick, so she took me to the vet. Everyone who works in the vet's office is a girl, and they like to fuss over me, so it was great. I felt a lot better after everyone petted me and gave me kissies and treats. The doctor said I was fine, so I knew the aliens didn't touch me.

When Mama took me home, I was still afraid to go in the house. I hid in the back yard until it was dark, and Mama said I looked like I had been chased by a poltergeist. I don't know what that means. Finally, I had to come in. At least the rat dogs who live next door didn't see how the aliens scared me; I would never have lived it down. Mama and I had a long talk, and she held me in the rocking chair for a while (I'm manly enough to talk about that now). Then Mama gave me a "calm down" pill, and I went to sleep. The aliens went away during the night, and the smoke alarm was fixed.

I felt a lot better by the next day, but even now if the smoke alarm goes off in the kitchen I will shake. Mama burned a piece of toast a few weeks ago, and she knew to hurry up and turn on the fan, and we went right to the rocking chair. No aliens can get you while you are in the rocking chair! I know that now.

Otherwise I am *very* brave. Besides the aliens from outer space, I am not afraid of a thing. I think that is pretty good for a brave (and did I mention handsome?) dog boy like me!

CHAPTER 3

THE OMELET IN THE CLOSET AND OTHER GOURMET SNACKS

I think you remember Grandma, that when I was little I used to like to get a special treat, like a fried egg on Sundays. Now I have Auntie Debra. She lives here with Mama and me, and she is a real chef and will make me anything I want. She even has checkered pants! Sometimes she is a little too pushy with those vegetables though, and I have to show her who is boss.

A couple of weeks ago, Mama went out on Sunday morning and brought back biscuit sandwiches. I ate the biscuit first, and then Mama gave me the bacon from another one, and after that was gone, she gave me the eggs. By that time they were all hard and rubbery, so I decided to save them for later. You never know when you might need a good snack hidden away for a rainy day, so sometimes when I don't have plastic bags, I bury cookies and treats under pillows or hide them under the bed.

Mama said the egg part was something called an omelet, so maybe that's why it was really easy to carry without losing a bite. I took it upstairs and hid it in Auntie Debra's closet. I figured she wouldn't find it for a long time—maybe days. But when Mama went in there in the dark after she folded the laundry, she stepped on it. She wasn't happy at all (I didn't know she could bark!), but the good part is that I haven't gotten any more rubber omelets.

I started liking bread after Mama gave me toast on Sunday mornings. Mama calls these "bread bones" 'cause I like to make them crunch. I also like any other kind of bread. When Auntie Debra was taking baking classes in chef school, I would sit by the counter in the kitchen whenever my sniffer told me she had come home with warm baked goods. They smelled *yummy*. If I cried a little bit and gave her the paw on her chef pants, I would get some, maybe a roll or even a pizza crust. They were great!

I like cookies too. The best ones are the molasses cookies Mama makes for our cousins. They are sooo good. I can't even stand to hide them and save them for later. I eat every single one right then and there!

As I said, I don't really like vegetables and won't eat them unless they are stuck to the good stuff, like meatballs or gravy. Why do people even bother with celery? I have eaten magazines and chew toys that taste better. Fruit isn't very interesting either. I think fruit that comes in balls, like apples and oranges, taste like tennis balls. Ugh.

I do have a favorite vegetable though—French fries! I looove French fries. I like sweet potato French fries too. I don't really like the fast-food ones very much. Those are okay when they are warm, but not afterward.

When it comes to food, I'm like my mama in a lot of ways. I think you can put cheese on anything and it will taste good. I very much like cheddar and Parmesan on spaghetti. Spaghetti is fun, and I like all the other kinds of pasta with red sauce too. I like tuna and noodles, but pasta treats are the most fun when Mama holds the noodles up in the air and I get to slurp them in.

Mama also knows I need protein, and that's a good thing because now that I'm a chef dog boy, I don't even bother with dog food. I like my steak done rare, thank you, and served in tiny bites. I'm very proper and have very good manners. I don't snap, and I don't grab. I like it best when Mama gives me meat one piece at a time or even on a fork.

I like fish too. It isn't just for cats anymore. I like salmon (if it's grilled and served with rice), tilapia, tuna, and shrimp. I like shrimp better if it's peeled.

Naturally, I do eat dog treats. Treats are different from regular old dog food. I especially like Beggin' Strips and bone cookies. Sometimes I like the cookies from dog bakeries—but not the sticky peanut butter kind. Yuk! The best treat I ever got was a real marrow bone. It was so good that my nub tail just couldn't stop wagging! Woo hoo! I saved that old bone, and every once in a while I will play with it again and remind myself just how good it was.

Treats can be educational too. Some nights Mama gets a handful of Cheerios and teaches me how to play catch by throwing them up in the air for me to catch them on my tongue. Right now I'm good for three out of every five. I need to practice more.

Truthfully, I like to eat whatever I smell cooking and whatever the people have! Sometimes Mama thinks I'm getting too picky. One night she picked me up and put me in the high chair. She didn't know that I would like it. I want to do it again!

Before you ask, I've been a good boy all month. I only shredded two magazines. They were boring. I've learned to *never* chew Auntie Debra's cooking magazines. She turns all red and puffy and hides the treats.

CHAPTER 4

BACK TO SCHOOL AND TO THE PET STORE

I've been thinking about going back to school—obedience school, that is. I was too immature when I went the first time, and I didn't do as well as I could have. I think I'm ready now to work hard and be the honor graduate.

I was still a puppy then, and we went to the classes in a pet store. It is a very big store for dogs and even cats and some birds. It has lots of smells in it, and they were very distracting. Big dogs walked by the area where the class was held, and little dogs rode past, sitting up in shopping carts. It was like being in a circus ring, and I was kind of dizzy from all the noise and smells. I didn't do well in any of the math lessons or in the "come to Mama" test at all.

One day when we went in, somebody had peed on one of the bone displays. You know what that means. Everyone else who went by had to add their own smells to it. Mama was standing there talking to one of the other owners while I was sniffing; it smelled like about three dogs had been there, so I could make a good contribution. I hiked my leg up and added to the fun. Unfortunately, I couldn't aim very well then and missed the display altogether and peed all over Mama's leg. She was not happy at all—especially because it went into her shoe. She squealed like a poodle! I laughed, but that was a big mistake. I got a stern talking to, as you might guess, but I learned that if I look innocent and lay my ears down, the scolding is over very quickly because Mama doesn't like to hurt my feelings.

That wasn't one of my better classes. This time I know I could do a lot better. I bet I can even do the tricks now. I've seen the dogs that do tricks on TV, and I know I could do better than they do.

I like to watch TV if there are dogs on. I watched part of the Puppy Bowl before Mama watched the Super Bowl. I especially liked watching those Lab puppies play in the water pan. They are really silly. My favorite movie is *Lady and the Tramp*. I know it's a cartoon movie, but I really like Tramp. I've seen it about three times, and Tramp is my hero. I like my hair cut like his. I could be a movie star. Really.

Last month Mama let me watch the Westminster dog show. I especially liked watching all the dogs run around that ring. I was really paying attention when a little Yorkie was put on the table by his owner and the judge looked at him. Then the owner gave him a treat and he dropped it. When that treat fell, I jumped off the couch and ran over to look under our TV in case it had landed there, but I couldn't find it. Mama laughed and laughed. I didn't see what was so funny because I'd been cheated out of a treat. Mama could tell

I was miffed, so she went to the kitchen and got me a biscuit from my treat jar. That made me feel better.

Since obedience school, we've only been back to that pet store a few times, and I used to go there to get a haircut. A bunch of high school girls work there, and they all have black hair and black fingernails. Mama says they are Goth girls, but I think they look like big spiders or vampires. They have black leather pants and rings in their noses. I think they are scary. After the last time, I asked Mama if we please could stay home, and she said I don't ever have to go back there for a haircut again. I get my hair cut at home now in the kitchen. It's not fun, but there are always rewards—and no Goth girls.

Mama cuts my hair on the kitchen butcher-block table. I don't like that name, but she says we don't butcher, we scalp. I don't like to be brushed, so sometimes I have a lot of matted hair on my legs and my haircut takes longer. Ugh. But this table is really high, so Mama knows I can't jump down and run away. Usually she holds me and talks to me and promises me treats while Auntie Debra cuts. The worst part is when they cut the hair under my tail. That razor vibrates, and when it gets too close to my very private parts, I just sit down. So sometimes I have a tail that Mama says looks like a flag hanging off the back end of a boat. This time she cut it short. It looks good.

After the haircut I always get a bath, which is kind of like double jeopardy, but it does feel good, and I look like Mister Handsome afterward. Because Mama and Auntie Debra have come to expect it, I do the crazy dog dance after my bath. I run in circles around the dining room, dash into the living room, jump onto the couch, and then head upstairs to roll on the bed. It doesn't matter how much I get dried by the towel; I still like to do the dance.

I'm very glad now that winter is over. Mama had let my hair get longer because it was so cold this winter, but then she said I looked like a cocker spaniel! Now I look like a schnauzer again, and that's good. If it gets cold again, I can wear my sweater.

I got a new sweater for Christmas this year; it's white with gray polka dots. It is sooo embarrassing to wear that. I like the Chia Pet sweater a lot better. I want it to stay warm. I got to lie in the sun on the deck yesterday, and it was great. Even better, Auntie Debra turned on the grill and cooked me a steak. Now this is what the good life is all about!

Next time I write, Mama wants me to tell you all about why she calls me Pinocchio. It isn't a very interesting story, but I will tell you anyway someday. At least my friends don't know that name.

This Sunday is Easter, and I know the Easter Bunny will bring me some brioche! Now I know what hanging out in the kitchen will get me. Last year I didn't even know what brioche was! I don't know why they want me to believe some rabbit is bringing it. I know Auntie Debra will make it in the oven.

CHAPTER 5

GIRL PEOPLE AND GIRL DOGS LIKE REAL BOYS

Girls like me, and I like girls! I like all kinds of girls. I like dog girls and people girls. I even like cat girls. Sophie is a cat, and she lives next door. She doesn't like me though, and I don't know why. Last week she let me get close, maybe because she was on her porch, and let me sniff her nose, but that was it. She ran away. This hurts my feelings because I've always been very nice and polite, but Mama says Sophie just doesn't trust dog boys.

There are lots of dog girls in our neighborhood. I like Dixie; she is a basset hound who lives across the street. She thinks I'm too barky, but Mama says that her big ears are very sensitive. I like Maddie, the black Lab who was my girlfriend until she got so big, and I like Roxie, who lives around the corner. Maddie always wants to make up and get back together, but I know she really just wants to come to my house and eat out of my dish. I think she has another boyfriend in the neighborhood. It's probably Rudy; he is big too. Roxie is part Greyhound and part something brown, so she is very fast. but she is not too tall and likes to play tag. When she wins, though, she wants to put her paw on my head and push it down. I don't much care for that, so when we wrestle, I always turn over and kick with my back feet. Mama says I have big rabbit feet, and that is one of my best wrestling moves.

Little people girls, though, are the best. I like to lick them and nibble on their ears. Sometimes they don't know how to play puppy games, so Mama has to show them how to play tag and share the ball. I especially like little girls with popsicles because they always let me have a lick or two, even if they don't mean to.

Grown-up people girls are even more fun. One of our new neighbors was sitting out on her front steps one day when we went for a walk. I stared at her until she noticed me, and when she said, "Hi, Benson!" I wagged my nub tail and slowly went up her steps and into her lap. She kept saying, "Oh my, you sweet little thing," so I knew she really liked me. She scratched my neck. The best part is always when I kiss them and nibble on their ears. I just love it when girls giggle! When the neighbor lady wasn't looking, I peeked in her shopping bag to see if she had any treats.

Mama says I'm a reincarnated gigolo. I don't know what "reincarnated" or "gigolo" mean; Mama says it's Italian for "handsome boy." I like Italian food, so that makes sense. Mama couldn't quite make me understand reincarnation, but her story is that when I was an angel, I went to Saint Peter and said, "I'll go back to Earth as a dog, but *only* if I get to live with people girls who wait on me hand and foot and fulfill my every need." Mama says when I got here to Virginia, she was there to greet me with new toys and a soft pillow. Then Auntie Debra came in and said, "Would you like a steak or grilled chicken?" I looked up to Saint Peter and whispered, "Thank you!" I don't remember any of this; I think Mama made it up. But if gigolo means handsome boy, well, I am all that—and a bag of chips!

I learned a long time ago there is always something for me in a shopping bag. After the first few times when treats magically appeared, I knew to look for them. One day Auntie Debra had bought a lot of groceries and brought them into the house in plastic bags. She put them up on the dining room table so they would be easy to unpack later. Then she went back out to the car to get the rest of the bags. I couldn't wait to see what was in there for me, so I got up on the chair and looked, but I still couldn't see. I hopped up on the table and was busy searching the bags when Auntie Debra came back in. She caught me with my head in the bag and came over and tweaked my nub tail!

I was going to tell you why Mama calls me Pinocchio. It is because I like boys too. Not in the same way I like girls, but I do like dog boys and cat boys and people boys. Actually, I've never met a cat boy. I like all the dog boys in our neighborhood except Smokey. Smokey is a spaniel, and when I was little, he called me names and tried to bite me. I always bark real loud now when I see him, but he has the nerve to look innocent and ignore me! It just makes me madder. I like everybody else.

I especially like ten-year-old boy people. They really know how to play—jump, run and fetch, shake the stick, tag, and a lot of other games. Only some boys know how to really play though. A lot of boys whose parents moved here from other countries live in our neighborhood, and some of them have never met a nice dog boy. Mama and I show them how to play, but they need a lot of work.

I lie on the back of the couch and look out the window when they play in the parking lot; I bark and cry to go out to play with them. Mama calls me Pinocchio then because she thinks I want to be a real boy. I know I already am!

CHAPTER 6

THE DARN POOP RULES

I'm thinking about running away. There are too darn many rules around here! Darn! (I like to say darn, especially because I'm not supposed to). Darn!

It's like this. The rule is I'm not allowed to bark on the deck. Well, the two little girls who live a few houses down go out on their deck and bark at me. How come I'm not allowed to bark back? It isn't fair.

I'm not allowed to eat chewies in bed. Mama says it makes too much noise when she is trying to sleep, and she doesn't like to wake up in the night to find I've propped an old bone on her shin to get a better grip on it. I still hide them under her pillow, though, after she goes to work in the morning. Ha!

The poop rules are the absolute worst. I get reminded about them every day. First, I'm not allowed to sniff other dogs' poop. I don't see why not. You can really tell a lot about a person—er, I mean dog—this way. You know, where they've walked, what they had for dinner last night, what kind of a day it's been.

After she says this big "no," Mama always has to throw in, "And you had better never eat any horse poop either." I don't know why she has to say that. I've never even seen any horse poop. Because she keeps bringing it up, now I *want* to eat some horse poop.

The worst of the poop rules, though, is that I'm not allowed to roll in deer poop. On one of our Sunday morning walks by the ball fields, Mama took off my leash early and let me run down the dirt road on the way in. While she was busy looking for the beaver, I saw some deer poop over by the big oak tree. Woo hoo! It sure smelled strong, but Grandma, it didn't smell any worse than some of that French cheese that Auntie Debra brings home. I swear, darn it. Because it smelled so good, I rolled in it. I've never done that before, so my aim wasn't really good, and I got most of it on my neck. It sure was great!

Every once in a while Mama reminds me I'm descended from wolves, and I thought I smelled wild that morning! I ran to show Mama I had rolled in deer poop and let her smell for herself. I thought she would be happy for me. I was wrong.

Mama scolded me all the way home, and she held onto only the very tippy edge of my leash. The rest of that day was awful. I got not one, but three baths, and afterward you could still smell the poop a little bit. I didn't get any Mama kissies for a week. Every time she looked at me, she would make a pickle face.

I bet Maddie is allowed to roll in deer poop, darn it.

Actually though, aside from the three poop rules, I guess it isn't so bad around here. Last night I got to sit in Mama's lap on the deck. I like that a lot because I can see onto the neighbors' decks and look down into their yards. I gave the rat dogs the evil eye and then watched for all the neighbor kids to run by. Some of the neighbor dogs strolled by too. Most of them don't get to sit on their mamas' laps out on the deck.

Auntie Debra grilled me a veal chop. Oh, and I'm supposed to tell you, you shouldn't worry about me eating any of the bad or recalled dog food. After the big scare with it, Mama said my lips would never touch dog food again. Good, I say!

Mama bought a fountain for our deck. It looks like an upside-down bee's nest, and it sits out by the grill and the water bubbles out of its top. I know spring is here when Mama turns on the fountain. She set it up last weekend, and as soon as it was bubbling, I took a drink out of it. I like to drink out of the fountain; no other dogs in our neighborhood get to do that.

I guess all of these rules aren't too bad. I don't even have to put my toys away when we have guests. I hate it when they step on my Cheerios, though, so I always try to eat them all.

Some nights after work, Mama gets a handful of Cheerios and sits on the steps, and we play catch. This is the only way I like to play catch. Mama throws one Cheerio up in the air, and I catch it in my mouth. She says now I have a pretty good batting average, whatever that means. I like to catch them! Sometimes I can get four in a row, and it makes me happy and my nub tail wags all by itself. Then I get a free one I don't have to work for. Mama just hands it to me. That's the best.

Well okay, I guess life is pretty good after all. And those poop rules aren't so bad. I just wish I could bark on the deck.

I'm sorry I said darn. I won't say it any more.

CHAPTER 7

DAYDREAM BELIEVER

I have a great idea for a new TV show. It would be called *Benson, the Spy-Wolf* and have lots of real adventures starring me! First I would defeat the Chinese-Siamese bulldog spies and then maybe Smokey, because I think he is from the Taliban. Don't you like my idea? I like it a lot. I could even have two assistants, like pugs, but they would have to be in the background. First I have to see if Mama will let me take karate lessons. I could do wrestling now, but I think for bad guys you have to be able to kick a lot.

Or wait. Maybe it should be a movie. What do you think, Grandma? I would like to be a movie star. But if I were on TV, I could have a new adventure every week. Yeah, TV is better I think. More is always better. At least that's what Auntie Debra always says after she has been shopping.

We have a new deck, and it is made of Trex, whatever that means. Mama likes Trex because she says it won't give me splinters in my toes and because I don't slide on it as much. She says it also drains water better, and I know she did that on purpose so I can't drink rainwater out of the cracks. I still drink more out of the fountain than from my water bowl in the house. Water just tastes better when you get it fresh and it is outside. Sometimes I drink out of the flower pots too, but Mama doesn't like that. I have a people drinking glass on the floor in the bathroom upstairs just in case I get thirsty in the middle of the night.

Our neighbor Sam built the new deck, and he let me help him. I like Sam a lot. I need a man to look up to, and Sam is a good person, even if he does like cats. He made sure I had a place every day where I could stand and check out everyone in the neighborhood. That was a good thing. Sam tells me secrets too. I know a lot now about vans and cats and power tools—all the things boys need to know. He promised to tell me about baseball too, but I already know about baseball from my walks with Mama to the ball fields.

Besides, baseball is really just another game of fetch. First someone throws the ball, and then there is an added step where someone hits the ball. Everyone then tries to fetch the ball while a couple of people run around in a big circle. Then they all jump up and down. It is still just "Fetch the Ball" though; I don't care what else they call it. You can't fool me.

I have better games to play, all of my special ones, and I have a secret cave to play in. Nobody knows about this but you, Grandma, and I know you won't tell. My secret cave is in Mama's bedroom under her bed. She has some rugs and old pillows under there, so I have to push them out of the way to make my secret place, but then I can crawl in and no one knows where I am. Sometimes I just daydream but I also play space rangers and sometimes I play cowboys in there, but lately all I want to play is *The Adventures of Benson, the Spy Wolf!* Mama calls my name sometimes when I've been in there a long time, but she always says she doesn't know where my secret place is! I know she can hear me though, because there are some "yip yip" sound effects you have to do when you play space rangers.

I do lots of thinking in there too. Lately I've been thinking about Sophie a lot. You remember me talking about Sophie; she is the cat girl next door who has Sam as her people. I really like Sophie. Yesterday I told Mama I want to marry Sophie when I grow up. She won't have anything to do with me though; maybe that's why I like her. I like girls who are hard to get. But Mama says Sophie won't ever want to marry me because we aren't the same species. I don't really believe that though. One of these days she will come around. It would be such a perfect relationship. Sophie is fast, and she can catch birds and squirrels and chipmunks and bring them home. Then we can play with them. I bet Sophie would like to play space rangers too—or maybe even *The Adventures of Benson, the Spy Wolf!*

28

Mama took a picture of me when I was having a nap on the couch in my new bed. My new bed is very soft! Mama says this is what I was thinking: "I dreamed I was on a cruise, a big cruise, and the butler knew exactly how I took my chewies!" Actually I was dreaming about *Benson, the Spy Wolf!*

PS: Next month is my birthday, and Mama says I can have a party! I'm going to invite all of my friends and some people too. We will have steak and bread bones. It will be great!

PPS: Mama's friend Cathy says eating horse poop is good for dogs, but in moderation, of course. It is actually like having a big bowl of yogurt! Her dog girls, Lady, Gracie, and Tippy, are going to take me to meet Emma when we visit them. Emma is a Welsh pony, and she is going to make us a treat!

CHAPTER 8

ME AND MY ALLOWANCE

First, I just want to say it was an accident. Just in case you hear something about it from someone else, I want to be the first to say it was an accident. I didn't mean to do it. Really.

You know how when people go to bed they fluff up their pillows? Well, I was on the bed and was trying to fluff up the bedspread to make a really good spot to lie down in. I scratched at it and scratched at it. I was going to turn around three times (it's a good luck thing) and lie down and stretch. By mistake, I scratched a hole in the top of the bedspread. It was an accident! The bad part was that Mama was right there, and she saw the whole thing. I didn't even get a chance to cover it up or blame anyone else.

Now Mama says I have to pay for a new bedspread out of my allowance. I don't have that much money in my allowance, Grandma! But that's because I ate three pairs of flip-flops last summer, and it took me a long time to pay those off. Now that I'm really mature, it is very discouraging to wonder how long it is going to take until I have enough money for a good vacation at the dog spa. Mama probably will want me to pay for the matching curtains and pillow covers and everything. It just isn't fair.

By the way, it isn't easy earning an allowance around here either. I have to lick the dishes every night before they go in the dishwasher. That isn't so bad, but sometimes they eat really yucky things, like peas. I do help Olga when she comes to clean the house. I don't chase the vacuum cleaner, and I always point out where there are nose marks on the windows. I just don't say whose nose marks they are. (Last week I stole Olga's flip-flops when she wasn't looking, but she found them and hid them in the closet—tee hee! I think Olga said a bad word in Spanish, but I'm not sure. All I know is "Hola, Benson!" That means, "Wag your nub tail.")

I also have to help Mama pull weeds in the backyard by the patio. I've even dug holes to look for the chipmunks who try to eat our garbage, but none of these jobs pay a lot.

Mama said maybe I ought to be a working dog. I know that there are all kinds of working dogs, not just Seeing Eye dogs like the golden retriever I saw one day going into the grocery store. (I was jealous—so much meat in one place.) Anyway, Mama said there are lots of German shepherd police dogs who work in the Pentagon, and they even get to wear badges. They don't ever have to eat peas or other bad things either, just sniff for them. Mama said they have Beagles at the airport who sniff out illegal fruit in people's luggage. I don't want to be just a sniffer. I think I have a lot more to offer than that.

My friends, the skinny white boys Opie and Que (they are bichons—Mama says that means moody in French), are going to be therapy dogs. That means they get to wear an orange vest and visit sick people in the hospital and get petted a lot. I think I would like that. Any job where all you do is get petted a lot would be a-okay with me! One time Aunt Tiffany (she's a dog walker, not a dog whisperer) put an assistance dog vest on me so I could go in a store with her. I was very proud and tried to look like a professional. She never told me what I was supposed to be assisting with. The whole time I was worried someone would ask me where the toothpaste was and I wouldn't be able to help, so I'm not sure about that. I don't like to carry a lot of bags either.

Maddie, of course, is a retriever, even though I don't think she's ever seen a duck unless it was on a plate. I don't think I would be good at retrieving stuff because of the swimming part. What I do best is guard the house. Nobody could ever sneak into our house because I am always watching. I lie on top of the sofa to look out the window at the neighborhood, and I patrol the deck to check out the backyard too. I look at everybody else's backyards too. Maybe I could get them to pay me something.

No bad guys could ever get by me! I can hear Mama's car when she comes home, and I can hear it when she is a whole block away. I tear through the house and sit by the front door and squeal until she comes in. Sometimes guarding involves long hours, and you don't get to rest much until all the lights go out and it is time for bed, but I like it, so it's a pretty good way to earn my allowance. Mama says I still have to learn that if they aren't bad guys, I don't need to bark at them.

After I realize the visitors or neighbors are good people, I don't really bark anyway. I squeal at them to pet me. Mama says it is a really embarrassing little poodle squeal. I don't care though; it works. I know too much barking cuts down on the petting, and I sure like the petting part. I'm going to ask Mama for a raise in my allowance! I think I've earned it.

Mama has lots of pictures of me on patrol. Don't you think I need a big badge, too? I want a sign for the house that says, "Beware of Guard Dog Boy". By the way, Grandma, it is now only two more weeks until my birthday party. I can't wait! Uh, oh. Mama is calling me. I've got to go now.

PS: It was an accident.

CHAPTER 9

BIRTHDAY SUITS AND BIRTHDAY PRESENTS

I don't see why I have to wear clothes. Auntie Debra has a bad habit of trying to put clothes on me. I have four sweaters, a raincoat with a hood, an overcoat that looks like Sherlock Holmes's, a University of Oregon cape (it's bright yellow!), a ski cap, a baseball hat, and the most embarrassing item of all—reindeer antlers to wear at Christmas. Ugh. She even bought me little boots for winter, but I've managed to run away every time she gets them out. I bet Auntie Debra would try to put a bathing suit on that beaver to go swimming in if she could. Grandma, I think you ought to tell her that fur is enough—or hair, in my case. Enough is enough!

I don't want to wear anything except the Chia Pet sweater, and then only if it is really, really cold and I've just had a haircut. Can you believe she wants me to wear goggles when we ride in the car? That's so I don't get a piece of dust in my eyes, she says. Well, I know how to blink! It is embarrassing to try to bark really big and bad at someone when you look like a geek.

I really like to ride in the car. I'm usually only allowed to put my nose out the window on the right side, and then only if there isn't any traffic. Mama won't let me poke it out at all when we go more than thirty miles per hour or travel on a four-lane highway. The absolute best parts about getting to put my head out the window is that I can smell a whole lot of things really fast and my ears flap and feel really cool when they blow back. I like to look at people in other cars, but I don't bark at them. I only bark at the ones who walk along the street or cross in front of us, especially if they are close enough to jump when I sneak a good bark up on them. Did you know people eat in their cars a lot? I think it is like being in a crate.

For my birthday, I got a special treat: to go in the car to meet Tippy and Gracie and Lady. They live on a farm near Madison, Virginia, where the horses live. On the way there, Mama let me look out the left window when we were at a stoplight. I saw a lot of very silly people who made faces at me. I think they were watching my ears go up and down as they made faces; I couldn't help it—they looked ridiculous. Next time I'm bringing the camera.

I really liked all of the girls. Guess what secret I learned? Tippy is a Beagle with housebreaking dyslexia. She doesn't do her business outside; she goes in the garage! (Ooops. Mama says I wasn't supposed to tell that and I shouldn't talk bad about the personal habits of other dogs). Anyway, Lady has her own swimming pool and, like other Lab girls I know, actually lies down in it to take a drink. Gracie thinks she is in charge, of course, because she is a miniature pinscher. We met Emma and the other horses, and they were the biggest creatures I've ever seen. I don't know if I really saw them though—I just saw big feet and a long neck. I didn't really eat any horse poop either. It smelled okay, but I like my other treats much more!

The best part of the whole trip, though, was that I got to meet Tom. Tom and Mama's friend Cathy own the farm, and Tom has a nice floppy hat and a big green wheelbarrow full of horse food! He took me for a walk and scratched my ears and said I was a very good boy and that I could come back any time I want. I like him a lot.

I was just exhausted after all the excitement of that trip, so I slept all the way home in the car. I had a lot of rabbit dreams too, probably because I was hoping to see rabbits at the farm. Gracie said they were all asleep, but if she wanted to, she could make them come out to meet us. You know, Grandma, I wish we had a barn too.

After we got home, it rained really hard, and Mama opened the front door so I could watch it rain through the screen. That was okay until some very loud thunder boomed near our roof. I blinked twice, flapped my ears, and turned right around and ran (I tried to walk and look unconcerned) over to Mama. I jumped in her lap and hid my head in her armpit. So much for that storm.

The next day, Auntie Debra wanted to make chicken spit on the grill. She has an electric spit stick and put a whole chicken on it. Well, I had never seen such a strange thing, and it made a big moaning noise as it went around and around. When I looked up, the chicken turned over and waved its arm at me. Auntie Debra hadn't pinned the wings down, and every time that chicken moved, it waved at me. Now I tell you, that just made me mad. I growled and growled, so Mama picked me up. I know she wanted me to see that it was just cooking, but the chicken waved again and made me madder. I didn't stop barking till Auntie Debra fixed its arms. Nobody disrespects me like that on my very own deck!

Oh, I meant to tell you all about my birthday! But first, thank you for sending me the very nice card and the whole five dollars. Mama said it was enough to pay for the bedspread (you remember, the one I scratched a hole in) and for some treats. We are going to the dog bakery this weekend, and I get to pick out my favorite treats. I also got to eat a steak on my birthday, and our neighbor Rich brought me a card and some peanut butter dog ice cream. That ice cream is some wonderful stuff; you can lick it and lick it, and it lasts a long time, until your tongue is frozen or until it melts on the deck. But the best birthday treat of all was that I got to visit Cathy and Tom and meet their girls. Mama said we can go back soon!

CHAPTER 10

MAMA'S GOT A BRAND NEW JOB

Lots of new people and dogs moved into our neighborhood this summer, and I have been busy meeting them all. There are even two schnauzer puppies who live up the hill from us, but I don't know them yet. One thing is bothering me though; none of these new people can get my name right. One new neighbor lady heard Mama calling me and thought my name was Dunstin. Where did that come from?

Pat, who lives across the street from us, always calls me Norman. Mama keeps telling him my name is Benson and not Norman, but Pat is kind of an older hippie guy who doesn't remember things very well. He has a ponytail, too, and Mama thinks it looks like my back end! And Pat waves his arms around, kind of like that chicken on the grill. Mama said he likes to do tai chi when he goes for a walk. I thought that was some kind of fried rice. It looks pretty ridiculous, if you ask me.

It gets worse. The other night Mama told this nice man who was watering his lawn that my name is Benson, and he thought she said *Betsy*! I don't look like a *Betsy*! No, no, no! I am a dog boy, but I wagged my nub tail anyway, just to show I would forgive him as long as he gets it right the next time.

I think we are finally done fixing things around the house. We got lots of things fixed and even more things cleaned (including me) in the last few months (and at least I didn't get fixed—tee hee). The icemaker works now, and the ceiling fans are all cleaned off. The dry-wall got spackled, and the dining and living rooms have new paint, and the patio is clean. Auntie Debra had to move my toy box so the painters could get to one of the walls, and she counted all of my toys. She says she lost count after forty. I know what you are thinking, Grandma. "That is a lot of toys." But every one is very special to me, and I need to keep them all. Mama says we might need to share some with some of the less fortunate dogs who don't have good Mamas to spoil them, but so far I can't think of any that I need to share. I had Mama take a picture of me with a few of my toys.

Our house looks very nice! Mama said one day we might move to a new house, but that won't be anytime soon. I like this house though. I have a good view out the window, and of course there is my deck, but one day I would like to live in a house that doesn't have a lot of stairs. I sure would like a larger living room so we could play catch and toy tug-of-war a lot easier. Sometimes Mama gets too rambunctious when she throws the ball and breaks things on the table.

Oh, and while we were fixing things, Auntie Debra replaced the doorbell too. She called me a funny name though; she said I was Pavlov's dog. I didn't know what that meant, so I looked it up. I don't think it's true that I'm conditioned to behave a certain way. I don't eat just because a bell rings.

I do know how things are supposed to happen. When the doorbell rings, people show up at our front door. It always happens that way. "Ring, ring" means people come to visit. When Auntie Debra was testing the new doorbell, she stood outside the front door and pushed the button. It rang. Naturally I barked, but nobody new showed up. Hmmm. Then Auntie Debra laughed and laughed. She kept saying, "It's me, Benson. It's just me." Well, of course I knew it was her. I just couldn't figure out where all of those other people went. I think she scared them away because she was laughing so hard.

This is the time of year when bugs and birds start to slow down before fall starts. I almost caught a bird the other day when it was taking a bath in my drinking fountain, and I'm thinking of asking Mama for some peanuts so I can try to lure a squirrel onto our deck. Last year I ate a fly too. It had buzzed around my head for a month, every time I went near the grill. When the days began to get shorter, I waited for my chance. I waited until the fly got tired and slow, and then when it flew right in front of me, I ate it. Mama didn't ask for any puppy kisses for days after that. And for a week, my only treats were mint-flavored cookies.

Mama sure has been on vacation a lot in the last couple of months too. I like that a lot, especially because when she doesn't go to work, she doesn't have to get up at 5 AM or come home after 7 PM. But getting up at 5 AM is way too early for me. I don't even want a treat or cookie then. If it is dark or cold out, I don't have any interest in going outside for a little walk. But when she is on a vacation day, we get up like normal people at 7 AM, and then we take a nice long and leisurely walk. Sometimes we have raisin toast. I spit the raisins out though; they aren't good for dogs. I would rather have bacon. Bacon is always better. And if Mama goes out during the day, it is usually to buy more treats for me.

I know that this month she goes back to work and that she has a new job. As long as it keeps me in meat, bread bones, and treats, I don't care what it is. I really wish she would consider getting another Jeep with cloth seats. They were a lot easier to sit on and look out the window. Those curved leather seats in the Volvo

41

are too hard to hold onto, and they smell kind of like the really expensive chewies, so I get hungry every time we go for a ride.

I just hope we get to sleep in for another hour and that she comes home early enough for a walk before dinner. I've been cheated out of way too much play time, not to mention sleep. And Auntie Debra is done with chef school, so she is going to look for a catering job. Again, I'm not too demanding. I just hope she gets lots of leftovers and smells like a bakery every day when she comes home. Now that will make your tail wag, I'll tell ya!

CHAPTER 11

WHY SHELTIES WILL NEVER RULE THE WORLD

So there I was, licking Mama's ears and biting her fingers to make her uncover her face and get out of bed. It was 7 AM last Sunday, and I wanted to go for my long walk. Mama kept trying to hide under the covers, but Benson the Spy Wolf can find her anywhere! Then she said, "Benson! Can't I even sleep in on my birthday?" Well, I really felt bad! I didn't know it was Mama's birthday (and it's not—she lied to me just to sleep for a few more moments). I knew she was faking when she started to laugh, so I bit her toes! Ha! Anyway, just in case her birthday does happen and I'm not prepared, I wrote Mama a poem. It goes like this:

Steak for dinner

Chicken for lunch

I like toys

But I love you a bunch!

You don't think it is too much about me, do you? I hope not. I wouldn't want anyone to think I was spoiled. I'm also going to give Mama a picture of me, just hanging out so she can see how I wait for her to come home.

I have some good news and some bad news. My girlfriend, Maddie, is moving to Boston soon with her mom! I just found out she is a Red Sox fan. I don't know which is worse—that Maddie is leaving or that she watches baseball. She also swims in the river and carries around a Frisbee named "Squirrel," so there is no telling what some folks do for hobbies. She says she will write to me, but I don't know whether a long-distance relationship will work.

That's my bad news. The good news is that I went to the vet for my checkup last week, and Doctor Kelly said I was *perfect*. I gained two more pounds in the last year, and I now weigh thirty pounds. The vet said, "He is all muscle." I was glad to hear that. I work out every day! Besides, when I am Benson, the Spy Wolf, I am very hunky, kind of like the Schwarzenegger of schnauzers. The vet did say I need to have my teeth cleaned, so I have to go back. You know, nothing can make it a fun visit. I don't care—not even chicken-flavored toothpaste makes brushing sound attractive. I will go. I guess. Doctor Kelly is very nice—of course, you know I have to have a girl vet. She is very good with dog boys, and I think she even likes cats. Last time we were there, Doctor Kelly told Auntie Debra that she likes my haircut.

I'm very sensitive about my ears, and I don't like the sound of that razor up close and personal, so the hair on my ears is very long. Doctor Kelly said she likes my fluffy ears; she thinks they are cute. Mama says I look like one of those snowboarders who wears a Norwegian ski cap—you know, the cap with the pigtails. I think that is not a nice thing to say, but I'm not sure. I think Mama says that because she used to have big ears too (I overheard her telling Auntie Debra). Hers got downsized. I'm glad nobody wants to downsize or clip mine; my ears keep me very warm at night. And I can always tell when somebody is coming.

The vet also told Auntie Debra that I am a very, very smart dog boy. Now, everybody knows that, I think. Because I'm so smart, I know it is a good idea to eavesdrop on people when they come to visit. You always learn good secrets when the people think you aren't listening. Mama's friend Mary Pat was here last month from Germany, and she always brings me treats, so I put my head in her purse and snorted while I was looking for them. People really love it when you snort on their wallet.

Anyway, Mama and Mary Pat sat on the deck, and Mary Pat talked about her dog, Chauncy. Chauncy is a sheltie, which means he can be fooled very easily by cats and smart dog boys. Sure enough, Mary Pat says her cat Missy will lure Chauncy into the bathroom with promises of a backrub, and Chauncy falls for that lie every time. He knows Missy will shut the door behind him, but he still goes in. Then Missy shuts the door, laughs, and says, "Sucker!" She flicks her tail, turns, and hops out the window, and Chauncy has to spend the whole day in the bathroom alone with nothing to eat but toilet paper. That is why shelties will never rule the world.

I'm smarter than any cat, and I thought this sounded like a pretty good idea, so I wanted to try it. Last Sunday Auntie Debra went into the downstairs bathroom looking for tissues because she had a runny nose. As soon as she went in, I shut the door with my paw. There isn't any window in that bathroom. I knew I had scored! But then Auntie Debra opened the door from the other side and walked out. Hmm. I have to work on this trick some more, Grandma, but now I know how to do it. I know what you are thinking, and I know I have to be good because Christmas is coming soon.

I'm going to start making my list for Santa, so I have to go. It's going to be long.

PS: I promise to let Mama sleep in on her birthday too. But this year she gets only one.

CHAPTER 12

MAMA GETS A SLEIGH RIDE

We haven't walked down the path in the woods for awhile now. Mama has been taking the shortcut across the big road, and then we go behind the church to get to the park with the ball fields. I know why too—Mama doesn't like spiders.

Last week we walked down the path, and Mama was waving her arm in front of us, just in case there were any spider webs across our path. They are usually too high for me, so I don't have to worry (tee hee). Anyway, Mama missed seeing one web and came face to face with a big fat spider. She squealed like a little girl puppy and tried to back up really fast, but she tripped over a tree root and plopped down on her butt. Because it had just rained, she started to slide. I tried to get out of the way, I swear, but when I ran, I was still on the leash, and it was wrapped around Mama's wrist. We looked like a horse pulling a sleigh. I gave Mama a ride all the way down that hill in the mud. I wish I had a camera then! We didn't walk long that Sunday. Mama seemed to be kind of grumpy and said she wasn't in the mood to walk much with cold mud stuck to her butt.

If I had seen the spider, I would have bitten it so it wouldn't crawl on Mama. I learned from eating that cicada a couple of months ago that munching on bugs is a lot like chewing gum. After the flavor is gone, there is no point to keep on chewing. Never ever swallow.

Still, Mama says that isn't why we haven't been back on the path. It is because our neighbors said there were reports that illegal aliens are living in the woods under the bridge. Aliens! You know how I feel about aliens. Mama said they aren't that kind of aliens, not the ones from outer space. but illegal aliens. *Hel-lo*! If aliens from outer space aren't illegal, they sure should be.

Anyway, Mama said the aliens are gone now, but I don't want to risk running into them, no matter what kind they are, so we have been going across the big road. Mama says she saw a coyote last week. I didn't see any coyote; I was busy sniffing some trash. Because I'm not allowed to sniff trash, I had to sneak it in really fast.

On the way back, we saw a Jack Russell terrier who was out without any leash or walking person. Mama called him over, and he came home with us. Auntie Debra took his collar off, and we called his vet. The vet called his family, and they came to get him. We got to play a lot first though. He sure was fast. We ran around and around the dining room table until I was good and tired. Jack ate some of my treats, and we played with my toys. We talked about Christmas too. He is going to get a new tug toy that is green and white. I want a giant chewie candy cane. I got one last year, and it lasted for days and days. I want some new squeaker toys too.

When Jack's mom came for him, I was ready for a nap, but he could have kept going—and he nipped at my nub tail too, Grandma! Well, Auntie Debra asked his mom what his name was, and she said Pup-pup. I think that is a dumb name for a dog boy. It is as bad as people who name their cat "Kitty." Duh. You would think they could try to think of something.

Nobody calls my mama "human"—at least not that I know of.

It's only a few weeks now till Christmas. I'm going to help make people cookies this weekend, and then we are going to make dog cookies too. I really like the ginger cookies my mama makes. They're almost as good as the beef-flavored dog cookies.

I hope you know I have been a very good boy this year, Grandma, and I haven't even chewed up too many magazines. I did let Mama sleep in on her birthday—all the way till 8 AM. I hope Santa will be good to me. I've started to watch for him every day. I want to bark at the reindeer.

CHAPTER 13

1001 PLACES TO PEE BEFORE YOU DIE

Mama said it is all about the journey, so I made some New Year's resolutions:

- To stop pulling on the leash when we go down the front steps
- To not eat too many snacks before dinner
- To bark less and lick more
- To be a good dog boy every day
- To ride in the car every weekend

I think those are easy enough for me to do, except maybe the part about being good every day. I might need to skip a few days just to take a break.

I did have a very nice Christmas, and I got a lot of good toys. I like bears a lot, and I got a new bear, but the moose you sent me was the best. Moosie is my new favorite. Mama said if my toy box pile gets more than four feet high, we will have to clean it out again and take some toys to the less fortunate doggies in the orphanage. Just the thought of giving up some of my toys gives me the shivers in my back leg. All I have to do is wiggle it a little, and Mama knows I'm upset. Then I get to sit in her lap where it is nice and warm, and I get petted. That's the best part.

The other night I had a nightmare about somebody breaking in to our house to steal my toys! It was awful! Mama said I was crying in my sleep and my paws were twitching. She woke me up and said everything would be all right. Afterward, we went downstairs to look at my toys, and after I saw they were all there, even the new ones under the Christmas tree, I felt a lot better. I counted them too. Sometimes I don't do well with the higher numbers, but then neither does Mama. I know she can't balance her checkbook because the bank says so, but I can count, and I know all of my toys by name. I even got a stuffed cicada for Christmas! I call him Crunchy, like the one I ate!

I have been working on my spelling, Grandma. I got a soft baby book for Christmas so I can learn to read. If I can read, I will have a new way to enjoy magazines—tee hee. Some words I can already spell. When Mama and Auntie Debra look at each other and say, "Do you think he wants to go o-u-t?" I know exactly what that means; it means out! I also know d-o-g and c-a-t and t-o-y. Every time Mama spells b-a-t-h, I start to worry because I know that soon I will need to r-u-n! You can always tell anyway because they whisper when they talk about baths.

I had my picture taken all fluffed up and brushed to look handsome for our Christmas party. Every time Mama is cold I have to wear a sweater, but at least for this I only had to wear a scarf. It was way too froufrou, though, with those little snowflakes on it. I think I look like a train robber, except maybe on the Polar Express. You can see that Mama brushed my legs so much that I look really funny. You don't think this scarf makes me look heavy, do you? Mama's friend Cathy said I'm starting to look chunky, but it is all that hair! Blue is a good color for me.

I was eavesdropping on Mama when she looking at one of her Christmas presents. She got a new book called *1001 Places to See Before You Die*. Well, my mouth was full of Christmas chewie candy cane, so I must have misheard her because I thought she said the book was *1001 Places to Pee Before You Die*. Now I could relate to that. I was really looking forward to seeing the pictures. I thought there would be a lot of interesting bushes and telephone poles and car tires, but it was all mountains and beaches. I don't think it is much fun to lift your leg on a beach. You just fall over in the sand. There were a lot of snowy places in that book too.

I don't like snow much because it freezes to my legs when they are all fluffy like this, and it sticks in my beard. Snow is okay though, except when it is really deep. There are no good places for a short dog boy to go then. I really don't like ice. I went outside last week and there was a lot of ice on our sidewalk. I sneezed and slid halfway down the block. That doesn't mean I need to wear boots though.

I was very happy I didn't get clothes for Christmas. I did get a new leash, and it is more like a halter, Mama says. I've seen people girls in halter tops, and they don't look anything like this. Mama says it is so I won't hurt my neck if I pull on the leash. Because I already have a resolution about pulling, I shouldn't need it. I don't like it much—it feels like I'm wearing a puppy trainer leash with all of these straps. After the leash goes on, I must look like a big piece of luggage with a handle in the middle of my back. It's kind of embarrassing. You can't be descended from wolves and run free in the wilderness if you look like a piece of luggage!

I've got to go now, Grandma. We are having some yummy steaks on the grill tonight because it is still not too cold out.

CHAPTER 14

MEETING ELIZABETH

I have been very bad. I broke all my New Year's resolutions, and I am so ashamed. First, I pulled on the leash, then ate cookies before dinner, and then acted like a dog. I am ashamed. I am ashamed because I have been acting like a *regular dog.*

What happened was this: I had an itch. It was on my front leg. I couldn't scratch it with my nails, so I licked it. That felt good, so I licked it some more. Then more. And more. Before I knew it, I was hypnotized by the act of licking, the rhythm, and the slurp. It gave me something to do that felt necessary. I was busy. I thought it was making a difference. Before I knew it, I had slumped into a stupor and half of the hair on my leg was gone. (I'm hiding it in this picture so you can't tell.) Mama was upset because by then it hurt, so I licked it to make it feel better, and that made it feel worse. Auntie Debra threatened me with Elizabeth. I'd never heard of Elizabeth, and frankly, I didn't care who she was. By then I was a licking addict. I couldn't stop, so—you guessed it—we went to the vet. I got some pills and cream, and Auntie Debra introduced me to Elizabeth.

Elizabeth is a collar, but not really a collar. Dr. Kelly said it is called an Elizabethan collar because it looks like the big collars people wore on their necks hundreds of years ago. Well they are ugly and I can see why people stopped wearing them but I don't see why they gave them to dogs.

Elizabeth is more like a lampshade I have to wear around my neck and head so I can't lick my leg. And, by the way, I can't lick anything else either, or even eat my dinner. I went into the living room and put Elizabeth on the ottoman. I got on my elbows and tried to pull her off, but it didn't work. I couldn't even play with my toys! I was so depressed. After a few days of cold turkey, though, I started to feel more like myself again. Whew! I guess I'm lucky I got out early.

Mama says that's what being obsessive/compulsive is like. She calls it OCD. We have neighbors Mama named "the OCDs," and I was afraid if I became like that, I would have to go live with them. It's not like they lick themselves or anything, but they like to do work things over and over. Every Saturday morning Mister OCD washes both of their cars and waxes them. Then he washes their golf clubs. If we go out in the car on Saturday mornings, Mama always says "Eeewww. It's dirty! It's filthy! Wash it some more!" One day she forgot the sunroof was open, and he heard her. Ha ha ha. She doesn't say it now.

Mister OCD also has a big leaf blower. If even one leaf touches his driveway, he runs out with his blower and pushes it into the street. Maddie says the leaves make the street slippery, but Mister OCD hates all the leaves. I promised to never fall into the licking trap again because I sure don't want to go live with the OCDs! They would probably try to give me a bath every week, right after they clean their cars!

After meeting Elizabeth, I don't think I believe in New Year's resolutions anymore. I know I said this year I wanted to bark less and lick more, but that sure isn't how I meant it. Since then, I haven't been doing all that well with the other resolutions either, especially the one about not eating too many treats before dinner. Oh well. I will start again next month.

By next month, Maddie will have moved away to Boston for real, so I have to start looking for a new girlfriend and really soon, too, because Valentine's Day is coming, and I want to have someone to share a chewie with. You remember how I told you that when I grow up I want to marry Sophie? She is the cat next door. Mama said it probably wouldn't work out, and now I'm starting to believe that might be true. A few weeks ago I invited Sophie over to watch a movie with me. *Lady and the Tramp* is still my favorite because Tramp looks like me! But Sophie would only come over if we could watch *Catwoman*. What fun is that? It turned out we couldn't agree on a movie, and she didn't want to watch the animal channel. She wanted to bring her catnip too; that is just like dipping snuff. So it didn't work out at all. She sat in the windowsill at her house and looked out at me, and I stood on the deck and just looked at her. I couldn't think of a thing to say. And all I could think about was *Catwoman*. Who wants to watch *Catwoman?*

Maybe we are from two different worlds, but I think after the weather changes in the spring and we can go outside, we will find a lot of things to agree on, like chasing birds. I think I should get her a subscription to *The Bark* magazine. That might help bring her around so she understands where I'm coming from. What do you think, Grandma?

I've got to sign off now. I need to go count my toys again. Auntie Debra gave some away to a needy little puppy, and I want to make sure I'm not missing any of the really good ones. You know what really chaps my dog lips? When she gives away one of my rawhide chews I've been working and working on. Right when it is all soft and pliable and ready for that final enjoyable chew session, she steps on it and squeals like it are a jellyfish or something. Out it goes. I sure wish I could reach the top of the trash can.

PS: Mama says I will have my very own Web site soon. I don't think it's a big deal or anything, unless girl dogs write to me for advice or if they want to date me. I know that lots will. Probably billions.

CHAPTER 15

KISS ME, I'M IRISH!

I'm confused. I always thought I was German and that I have a nub tail and beard because I am a schnauzer, but now I'm just not sure. You see, Mama started looking on her computer last year to find out her bloodline. I can understand that because I know my dog ancestors back for a couple of generations. They all have very important sounding names, too, so I can understand Mama wanting to know if she is a special breed. After a while, I could hear Mama muttering about her grandparents and great-grandparents, and I think it is because she found out she isn't even purebred. Finally, she turned to me and said, "Benson, we are Irish! Well, mostly anyway."

Grandma, does that mean Mama is a mutt—uh, I meant to say mixed breed? Or that I'm Irish too? If so, I can get a button that says "Kiss me, I'm Irish" to wear when we go out for our long walks. Tee hee, just kidding. I don't think I'm Irish. I don't look anything like those people in all of Mama's old pictures. Mama doesn't either, not really. Except that they all have these really big ears.

Mama has fun doing this, and it keeps her busy, so it is okay with me. When she plays on the computer, I lie on my back on the futon with my head over the edge and look at her upside down, growling a lot. When Mama turns around, I stop growling immediately and try to look innocent. We play this game for awhile until she comes over and tugs at my beard and we go outside. After all, she shouldn't spend too much time on that computer. It isn't good for her.

Guess what I look for on our walks now? Christmas trees. There are at least four houses in our neighborhood that still have their Christmas trees up. I just can't understand why that is. I asked Mama about it because I don't see why you would keep a tree inside if it isn't going to grow and if you aren't going to get any more presents for a whole year! Some don't have ornaments on them anymore, but one still does, and every once in awhile, they turn it on. Maybe the people are lazy, or maybe they are going to pretend that they meant to leave them up and call them Easter trees. Mama says we will look to see if they hang eggs on them.

Last weekend we came back from a walk, and Auntie Debra had baked me a great big soup bone. Sometimes you just get the urge for a really good soup bone, you know what I mean? That's the kind of treat you need after you have had to go for a walk when it is raining. I don't like to go out in the rain. No matter how badly I have to go, I hate to get wet. I don't know what is worse really—wearing a bright yellow raincoat or getting my back all wet. So I won't go out unless Mama goes with me. After all, I think we should share the misery of getting cold raindrops on us. Otherwise I can cross my hairy little dog legs and wait all day. Sometimes Mama will let me go out the back door for a little pit stop on the patio. That is okay except that I think I won't get wet in the rain, and then when I least expect it, a great big drip drop lands right on the back of my neck. Ewww, that is just awful.

CHAPTER 16

PIRATES OF THE CARIBBEAN

I hurt my mama, and it was awful. I didn't mean to do it either. I really didn't. Mama had just come home from work, and I was doing the Welcome Home dance. (You remember; that's the dance where I squeal and jump and show the toy so the humans know I'm happy to see them again.) I don't think it is a lot of fun, but they seem to expect it. Mama likes it when I run off with her gloves and then stand on the back of the couch so I can lick her face, so I usually give her a pretty good show.

This time Mama lay down on the floor and expected me to run back and forth and jump over her while yelling, "Yay, my mama's home!" Like I said, it makes her happy, so I was doing it, but there was a horrible accident. My paw slipped, and I smacked Mama right in the eye. It must have really hurt because Mama screamed. I hid on the other side of the room, behind Auntie Debra.

Mama had a broken blood vessel in her eye, and it was all scary, horror-movie red. The outside part was all purple and blue. She kept looking in the mirror and saying something about *Pirates of the Caribbean*. Mama got checked out the next day by her vet, and he said she was okay. Mama knew I still felt bad, so when she came back from the vet, she lay down on the bed, and I inspected and sniffed her face very carefully. Then I licked her eye to make it better. It was kind of a big apology, even though I didn't mean to hurt Mama, and of course, Mama understood. She is the best at that. I got a chewie, so I knew everything was okay. I'm very careful now.

I love chewies and all treats. The best treat moment for me is one that is self-serve. Mama usually gives me about three treat sausage rolls for breakfast, and I try to save one for later. Around midmorning when I'm done patrolling the deck and doing guard duty at the front window, I can just reach into one of my special hiding places (it is usually the third cushion on the couch) for that hidden chewie. They taste so much better that way! Of course, the bacon ones are best in the morning, but I think a few of the marrow bones should be mixed in for variety. After all, Mama likes mixed nuts, and that is the same thing.

In truth, chewies are good any time. In the evening, Mama likes to have a handful of chocolate chips—you know, like the kind you put in cookies. (Personally, I would like to see her catch them when I throw them up in the air, but I don't think she would go for that). While she has her treat, I get a dog cookie or two as my treat. That is the best thing to have as a bedtime snack, especially the chicken drumsticks. Those are the bomb!

This weekend Mama wants me to enter the Milk Bone Moments contest. Of course I will win because I am the best looking boy out there. It probably isn't even fair to every other dog boy in the entire world that I want to enter, but I think I will anyway. I will make a great Milk Bone spokes-dog boy. I don't know though. If they want me to be groomed I might have to turn it down. If I look too froufrou, it would ruin my image with the girls in the neighborhood.

Did I tell you that Mama calls me "The Benson B"? Sometimes she just calls me "The B." I really like that; it makes me sound really grown up, don't you think? Some nice girl dog in our neighborhood could say to her mom, "Let's go out now! I promised The B I would meet him at the corner." I think it sounds really cool. Now that it is light later in the afternoon, I get to see more of the girls in the neighborhood.

Soon all of those girls will be writing to me. Mama and Chauncey's mom made me a Web site. It is called http://www.simplesite.com/Bensonsletters The site is very exciting because it features lots of stories about me, and it even has a mailbox so cat and dog and even people girls can send me love letters. So far, Auntie Melissa has written to me, and Chauncy and Brandi have too. I even heard from Cody—he is on the road now with his career as a show dog. Or is it Dobie? I spelled that wrong the first time and called him Doobie, and Mama said that was something else entirely. A very cute shih tzu named Rosie wrote me a nice note, too, and I don't even know her! Mama said it is a real dog blog!

If I am really lucky, maybe Sophie will send me a nice love note on my Web site. But Grandma, after my last letter when I talked about how Sophie wouldn't go out on a date with me, she was really mean. You know, mean like only a cat can be. Sophie wrote me an e-mail and said she would never go out with me and she wasn't going to come down off her pedestal and that I had dog breath. She said I needed to eat a fish mint!

CHAPTER 17

SPY WOLF COMIC BOOKS: 25 CENTS!

Benson the Spy Wolf was alert and ready for action. He pressed his back into the fallen tree, adjusted the camouflage netting, and felt his paw tighten on the laser gun. He knew the aliens were nearby, and Princess Sophie was their prisoner. The Spy Wolf was charged. He would rescue her!

He quickly scanned the path ahead with his binoculars. There was nothing to see but leaves and stillness. Not a rabbit moved. Not a squirrel. The Spy Wolf's eyes narrowed, and he flexed the broad muscles of his handsome chest. Benson knew how tricky the evil aliens could be. They could even send a black Lab to try to distract him with its silly games. Fetch a duck! Who could think about fetching a stuffed duck when aliens were lurking around every bush or boulder? He snorted. No, nothing could distract Benson, the hero of a million adventures throughout the universe.

Benson checked his supplies again. His backpack with its special air jets was ready in case he needed to blast away above the trees. Vroom! Vroom! Two cans of tuna (packed in water) were nestled inside his pack in case the lovely Sophie was hungry after he rescued her. He also carried a bottle of water and some catnip in case the evil aliens had drugged her against her will and she needed to be awakened. Of course she would need to be awakened! Then she could see her rescuer was none other than the legendary (and very handsome) Spy Wolf!

Benson sighed happily at the thought. Princess Sophie would be ever so grateful to him for rescuing her that she would come over to visit, and they would watch *Lady and the Tramp*. They would eat spaghetti, too, just like in the movie. He smiled at the thought and, well, drooled a little bit too. It was spring, and in the spring, the Spy Wolf's thoughts turned to spaghetti.

A whistle shattered his daydream.

Grandma, the whole story had to be put on hold because when Mama whistles for me I had better hustle! I ran out from the brush and left the aliens behind because Mama was getting pretty far away, and I sure didn't want to be left behind in those big woods. Maybe next week I will go back and rescue Sophie and destroy all the aliens. Yeah, before they can set off that smoke alarm.

Grandma, I have a question. We didn't get much grammar instruction in obedience school. When I rescue Sophie, should I say, "It is I, Benson, your prince!" Or should I say, "It's me, the legendary Spy Wolf!" or "Yo, Soph, let's go!"?

Mama is very pleased I don't need a leash when we walk in the woods on Sunday mornings because I come when she whistles. I'm very well behaved. Sometimes, though, when it is cold on those early morning walks, Mama can't make her lips work, and her whistle sounds like a squeak toy with a hole in it. I'm glad it is getting warmer out now, even though there are some big briars growing in the woods.

Last week we saw four deer. They looked like very big dogs. I would have chased them, but they were on the other side of the creek, and I would have had to get my feet wet to get closer. I think Mama should build a bridge for me. You know I'm not going in that water—that's where the beaver lives!

I have a new favorite thing to do in the bedroom. It is even better than eating a chewie on the bed when no one is looking! I like to sit on the bed and look at that most handsome of all schnauzers in the mirror. It is even better when Mama gives me kissies because not only do I get all the kissies, but I also get to watch that handsome Spy Wolf—*me*—get them too! Tee hee!

Those two schnauzer boys who live down the hill, Oreo and Bandit, are in obedience school. I heard their mom say they have to be separated because they won't behave in class. I guess maybe my record will be broken. That's only because there are two of them, those barker brothers. Mama read my letter to you, and she says I am very much in love with myself. That isn't true. Not really. Just because I like to look in the mirror and I am very handsome doesn't mean I'm stuck up or anything. Really.

PS: My Web site has had thousands and thousands of visits, and lots of girl dogs are writing to me. Some I haven't even sniffed yet! Chauncy is doing all the work on it. He has a lot of spare time since he has moved back from Germany and doesn't spend all day locked in the bathroom like he did there. Tee hee!

CHAPTER 18

LIKE, YOU KNOW, WOW!

Last Saturday, Mama came home from the farmers market, and she smelled like another dog! I sniffed her up and down, let me tell you. She said a very nice lady at the market had five schnauzer puppy-babies with her. They were ten weeks old, and one was a little girl named Pink. I had been thinking about asking Mama for a baby sister for my birthday this year, but now I've changed my mind. I want a skateboard instead.

I could see the future very clearly as I sniffed Mama's sweat-shirt. It wasn't pretty. This puppy-baby would come in and get *all* the attention, and she would touch my toys—then take them, and maybe even slobber on them. Ewww! Then she would want to sleep in my bed with Mama and me and would probably cry if she didn't get her way. Then she would probably try to steal my dinner! It isn't like I know this from experience or anything, but I sure don't like the idea of sharing my mama. I was here first!

Mama says I'm starting to act like an adolescent. I don't know what she means by that, but she says I'm not allowed to use certain words anymore. You remember that I'm not allowed to say d-a-r-n, right? Now I'm not allowed to say l-i-k-e or g-o either. This isn't fair because you use both of those words a lot, right, Grandma? You need them every day, huh, Granddad?

When Mama said that, I, like, gave her the look that says, "Whatever!" and walked out onto the deck so I could lie in the sun and make faces at the rat dogs. Then Mama, like, she goes, "Benson, come back here!" Ha! Like I ever come when I'm called the first time. So I, like, lie down on the deck and point my nub tail toward the screen door. Let her talk to the tail!

Just because Mama gets to tell people what to do all week long doesn't mean she can come home and expect me to, like, salute or something. I don't know. What is the big deal about being an adolescent anyway? I watch all the neighbor boys on their skateboards, and they are adolescents. I think. They all like me, and I'm still one of them. Robby said I can be in his crew at the middle school anytime. But yesterday he changed his mind. I was on deck patrol, and the boys were playing hide-and-seek. I barked when one of them went by and gave away his hiding place. Tee hee!

Maybe Mama is on my case (I don't know what that means, but the neighborhood boys say it all the time) because I like older girls, like Sophie, you know? I also like Ginger. Ginger usually goes out at about the same time I do in the morning, between 6:30 AM and 7 AM. Ginger looks like Lassie, but she has blue eyes and is kind of like the Nicole Kidman of collies, you know? She is always cool and never barks or anything. You should see her walk! She can sure move that tail. Some days she doesn't even speak to me. She just nods and goes on by. That just makes me bark all the more, especially if she won't look at me. When she's around, my voice gets all high and squeaky. I don't know why it does that. It's kind of embarrassing.

I always squeak with happiness when I see Rich. He lives down the street with Betty (who goes to work too early), so I see him outside on my first walk in the morning. Rich always talks to me and says to Mama that I have "turned out so nice!" I think that makes me sound like I was a cookie baking in the oven or something, but I know he means I am very grown up now. Every time I see Rich, I run to him, and he rubs my ears. Rich is retired, so he has lots of time to rub my ears. But the best part is that Rich always smells good, and if he gives me a good rub, I smell like his aftershave too. I like that a lot. I don't know the name of it, but it is probably called something like "Man about Town" or "Best Man."

It seems like it might have been a mistake to tell Mama to talk to the tail. I think I might get dog chow for dinner tonight instead of leftover steak. I did get to talk to Sophie while I was out there. I told her about my alien fantasy and that I would rescue

70

her. You should never tell girls you have dreams or fantasies about them, Mama says. Sophie sent me pictures at my Web site of what she thinks the aliens look like. Grandma, she is, like, *so* wrong. None of her aliens look like real aliens. I think they all look like animals in Halloween costumes. I'm really suspicious because Sophie said they all were some form of dog. Dogs are not aliens, even if they are from Venus and cats are from Mars.

Grandma, who could resist my special smile? Doesn't my sweet little beard face just make you want to hand over your steak and sweet potato French fries? Like, right now? That's what I'm talking about!

CHAPTER 19

THERE IS A DOG IN MY HOUSE!

I threw up! That's really all the big news there is from here—I threw up. Actually, I threw up three times. The first time I had jumped on the bed to tell Mama I really didn't feel well, and before I knew it, I threw up on Mama. Mama was asleep, so she didn't know. Mama can sleep through anything. Then I jumped down off the bed and threw up two more times on the floor. It was right by the bed, so Mama saw it first thing in the morning. Or maybe she saw the other one on the bedspread by her head first. I don't know.

I think I threw up because I ate dog food, and it isn't good for you. Just the thought of dog food now is enough to make me gulp a little. I haven't eaten any in years, so I don't know why I thought it would be a good idea now, except I was having this "green" problem. That's what Mama calls it.

You see, one of Mama's friends has a "furry farm," and she helps cats and dogs find good homes. Well, they found a schnauzer who needed a home, so they thought Mama might want this little girl dog to come live with me. Not! Mama is a big softie, and she felt badly for this little girl schnauzer who had lost her first family, so Mama drove all the way to Salem, Virginia, to pick her up. Her name is Maggie, and Mama calls her Maggie Moo. She is three years old.

Maggie has very bad breath and leaks on the floor when she gets excited. It's not that I'm jealous or anything—I like her just fine. I just don't want her in *my* house. She came here last Monday and has been working on every one of my favorite special chewies ever since. She touches my toys. She barks all the time. She has a bad haircut. She leaks. Other than that, I really do like her, even if she did put her lips on a Beggin' Strip that was in my mouth at the time. I told her to never ever do that again. I think she got the message.

The only thing I really mind is that she wants to sit in Mama's lap all the time. That is my place. Mine. Mine alone. This awful visit went on all week long. By Friday, I was really tired of her and her bad breath, and I thought it was time for her to leave. She eats out of a bowl, like a dog, and when Mama gave me some steak, she gave Maggie some too. Imagine that dog wanting to eat steak like I do. When she was done, there was still some steak left, mixed in with that icky, yucky dog food, so I ate it because I was mad.

Even at the time, I knew it was wrong—not that it was wrong to eat the rest of Maggie's dog dinner, but it was wrong that I put my head in a bowl on the floor and chomped away at kibbles or nuggets or whatever they are. I was sooo ashamed. I ate dog food, and I think it made me sick. That's my story, and I'm sticking to it.

Grandma, this is all so awful. I bet Mama will want me to sit there with Maggie and have our pictures taken for a Christmas card or something. All of the neighbors—who are *my* friends, by the way—want to talk to her and pet her when we go out for a walk. Not one of them talks to me first anymore.

Sometimes Mama sings her silly song:

Benson and Maggie sitting in the tree!
B-A–R-K-I-N-G!

At least she doesn't have any more lines for it yet.

On Sunday, I hid in my Spy Wolf cave and cried. I didn't even get to have my special place all to myself because Maggie tried to come in to see if I had any chewies hidden in there. It just isn't fair! Won't anything ever be the same again? Why can't she find another home? I could run an ad in the paper for her and everything.

I'm really sorry I ever said anything about a baby sister. I wish I had a skateboard instead.

CHAPTER 20

THE PAINT CAN CAPER!

The Intruder got me in trouble with my mama! It was awful, awful, awful. Now that Maggie's been here a whole month, she's starting to get real uppity, and sometimes she even tries to boss me around. Like that could ever happen! She is *not* the boss of me! She already steals my chewies and thinks I'm ready to play any old time she feels like it. "Well, it just doesn't work that way, young lady," I tell her. She just doesn't listen. I wonder if that is a schnauzer trait. Mama says it is.

Last week Mama had a new project. She was going to refinish the breakfast table and chairs we have in the kitchen and put new cushions on them. Before you even ask, I didn't do anything to the cushions. Mama spilled coffee on one of them, so she decided it was time to finally fix the chairs and the table and the benches. This is one of those furniture projects Mama has put off for years, so she needs to get on with it. Last Thursday, Mama stripped the old finish off the chairs. I've seen these home improvement projects before, so I told the Intruder to make sure she didn't sniff any of the chemical stripper.

Maggie Moo has a very small head, and that means she has a very small brain. Of course, she didn't listen to my wisdom about keeping her snout to herself, and she sniffed the stripper can. She got a headache, and Mama scolded her. After she chewed on one of Mama's new paintbrushes, she got scolded again so she ran inside. It was great that she left; I shut the door behind her, just like Chauncy taught me. Ha! All of us grown-ups got to stay out on the patio. I helped Mama by pulling weeds over by the trash cans. More allowance money just for me! For weeks now, I've had my eye on this big, brown rawhide stick dipped in beef gravy! I just need a few more pennies.

By Friday, Mama was ready to finish the chairs. She had decided to paint the legs white and put a dark coat of stain on the top parts. She got out her little stool and opened the paint can. We had already been for our first morning walk, and the Intruder was inside burping over her *third* Beggin' Strip. I was helping Mama again. After Mama stirred the paint, she started brushing the legs. Maggie must have learned a few of my tricks because she opened up the back door with her skinny little paw and came prancing out. She likes to get all barky and play chase games first thing in the morning. Not me. I'm like Mama. I want to wake up slowly and take my time. The Intruder came bouncing over to where I was sitting by Mama, just soaking in the early morning sun on my long and fluffy ears.

Little Missy yapped and huffed and barked, and then she got down into the playtime stance. It woke me up from my sweet morning daydream, Grandma. I was really surprised. In fact, I jumped. When I jumped up, my paw came down right in that can of white paint! I squealed because it was cold, and I jumped again. The paint can went flying, and I ran to the other side of the patio. When I looked back, there were white paw prints all over the pretty red bricks, and white paint was *everywhere*. It was between my eyebrows, on Maggie's butt, and all over Mama. Mama was surprised too. All she could say was, "Oh!" By then I was pointing at the Intruder because it was all her fault. And she tried to look sooo innocent.

As you might guess, it was a long morning at our house. I got a bath to clean my feet and then another one because there was still more stuff in between the pads on my front paws. Maggie didn't get a bath at all, which is really no fair. Grandma, I think she was laughing while Mama was cleaning my beard. She kept making snide remarks about how white it looked. Humph.

I know she looks innocent, but it is all a lie! Here she is, right after the paint can caper, as Mama calls it. I think she is laughing!

CHAPTER 21

DOGPOD CHILLIN'

It seems like the dog days of summer just got here. Why do they have to leave so soon? I was really enjoying all of my quality time on the deck. Mama grillin', and me chillin'. The smell of steak in the air is simply the best!

You probably can't see the headphones in this picture, but I have my dogPod on and am chillin', just listening to my favorite music. I have to do that because Maggie the Yapper is always talking in my ear these days, and you wouldn't believe it, Grandma, but she is a real little gossip mongrel. The things she says about that hound Prancer up the street would curl my tail if I had one.

Speaking of Maggie, if she doesn't stop eating so much, soon she is going to turn into Mega-Maggie. Tee hee!

I like to listen to music. Mama bought me a CD she thought she would play for me when she has to go out to the store to buy meat. It is called, *Songs That Make Dogs Happy*, but I think it's just silly. One of the songs on it says nothing but "You are a good dog" over and over. I already know that, so I didn't see any reason to download those songs. I do have my favorites though. One is "Born to Run." That is my theme song, and my other favorite is "Bad to the Bone." Of course, I am built like a very handsome "Brick House" too! I don't like rap very much—it sounds too much like barking. I boycotted Snoop Dogg after I found out he wasn't a real dog.

After Maddie moved away, I deleted "Hold Me, Thrill Me, Lick Me." Speaking of Maddie, you wouldn't believe how many times I've called Maggie "Maddie" by mistake. That pinhead is in a class by herself though. I've realized she is here to stay, but I sure don't know what they see in her. She yaps, she leaks on the floor when new people come to visit, and all she wants to do is eat. She does play okay, and as long as she doesn't scare away my girlfriend-to-be Sophie, I guess she is okay. Oh, I put some music on the dogPod for Sophie too—she likes the Pussycat Dolls.

The only really bad thing about Maggie is that she is ruining all of my toys. She is tearing them apart one by one. So far, the chicken has lost his head, the pony his cowboy hat, and the dinosaur an eyeball. The piggie lost just about everything. The bad part is that the chicken still talks, so Mama is keeping it in the toy box. It sure looks awful.

Maggie scatters my toys everywhere too. She has a stash on the landing and in each bedroom. There is a chewie with each pile of body parts. Mama says that makes Maggie feel like she is in doggie heaven. Well, I hate to tell her the truth, but this is my heaven, and she only gets to stay because Mama thinks she is a play dog for me. That's the truth, and everyone knows it.

This afternoon I'm going to switch from lying on the deck to lying by the front door so I can watch the kids come home from school. School started this week, and they all look so sad that I'm glad I decided not to go. They have to get up really early to stand on the corner and wait for the bus. I don't like the bus. It is loud, and the windows are up too high so you can't see very well.

I think I will stay on the deck with my dogPod. With all of the kids gone, the neighborhood is much quieter, and if that Moo stays inside for awhile, I can get in a peaceful nap without her chewing on my ears. She thinks she is staying inside because she will get all of Auntie Debra's attention, but really, Auntie Debra is giving me a break.

I know who's large and in charge. It's always me!

CHAPTER 22

MAGGIE HAS HER SAY

Maggie looked over my shoulder when I wrote you the last letter, and she is really mad because she thinks her side of the story isn't being told. I think actually she was mad because I called her "Mega Maggie" but honestly, Grandma, you should see her eat! I did say I was sorry afterward. Really, I did.

Now Maggie wants to talk to you, just like she wants everything else I have, so here she is.

> *Hi, Grandma. Hi, Granddad. Will you be my grandma and granddad? I don't really know what that means, but Benson says you love him, so I want you to love me too. I want everything he has. I'm still new here, but this is my home now and I want to fit in. I have two questions for you. 1) What are you having for dinner tonight? 2) Has anything really tasty rolled under your refrigerator lately? I could help out with that and with any other leftovers you might have. Benson has the job of deck patrol and house security, but I am a great vacuum cleaner. Just ask anyone. I can CLEAN UP.*

OK, that's enough from Maggie. After all, it is still all about me. Last time Mama went on vacation, she brought the Moo a present. My present was a stuffed husky dog, and hers was a rubber squeak toy. I really don't like rubber squeak toys; they feel icky-slippery on my teeth, and they are too loud. Mama brought Maggie a rubber crab, and she just carries it around the house by one leg. Ick. Maggie doesn't like the noise either. Sometimes Mama squeaks it at her just to make her mad. Maggie's lower lip quivers with each squeeze.

I got an even better new toy this week. This is how it all started. Mama's friend Cathy said because I am so very smart I would probably like to do dog agility trials. I didn't like that idea at first when Mama mentioned it because it included the word "trial," and all I could think about was O.J. I told Mama I wasn't interested. Then we started watching that TV show, *The Greatest American Dog*. It is another of those reality shows like Auntie Debra usually watches on the cooking channel, but this one is about owners and dogs—all kinds of dogs.

I got hooked on watching it. It was sad that the schnauzer got eliminated early on, but after that I cheered for the Maltese every week because he was a little guy. Most of the others were big dogs. I bet they smelled.

Each week they have to do challenges. These go way beyond tricks and walks and begging, and there are lots of obstacle courses. A couple of weeks ago, there was even a charging elephant! I think I would run from the elephant, and I know Maggie would take its banana, but I did like all of the ramps and jumps and tunnels and other playground toys. Mama said competition is what agility trials mean, so I was interested. I watched very closely, and most of those dogs got treats to go through the trials, and all of them got praised a lot for their efforts. I like that idea!

So Mama got a catalog, and this week my new red tunnel came in the mail! We tested it out in the backyard last night. I was very proud that I ran all the way through it and got a sweet little treat at the end! I am very smart and brave! Then Mama put up the jump. It looks just like the jump that horses jump over when they race, and I knew I could do it because sometimes I jump over the little parking lot fence when Mama and I go down to the ball fields for our Sunday walks. So Mama put it together, and I looked at it. Then I sat down. (I wanted Mama to say, "Pretty please." Tee hee.) Finally Mama got the idea and did say that. Then she ran and jumped over the rail, so I jumped over it too. I did it as many times as Mama did because I didn't want her to be eliminated. It was a lot of fun, and Mama says we can show it to all the dog boys and girls who come visit me for play dates.

Oh, and Maggie was scared of it, so she ran upstairs and hid. Actually, I think she laid down on the bed and painted her toenails. She is such a girl!

> *That is NOT true. I just didn't feel like jumping! If I had wanted to jump, I would jump. Boys! You just can't count on them to get the story right. He needs to remember what's mine is mine, and what's his is mine!*

Anyway, Grandma, if you were wondering who is still in charge here, it is still me. Here I am in my commander hat on the front steps. I give orders too!

CHAPTER 23

TATTLETALES TELL NO LIES

I don't care what anybody tells you. I am not a tattletale. I tell only true things, even if some people and dogs don't like to hear the truth. Ha! See, check it out. Here is a picture of my favorite piggy. No eyes. No legs. One arm. One ear. No tail.

As you can see, my piggy has problems. Piggy used to have two ears, two arms, two eyes, two legs, and one very curly tail. I like Piggy a lot because he has a tennis ball inside and bounces really well when you play catch. What happened to my piggy, you ask? Maggie did, that's what.

A whole bunch of my toys are now missing arms and legs and tails. Piggy probably looks the worst of all of them. From behind, you can even see his ball sticking out. The worst part is, as I pointed out to Mama, there aren't any ears on the couch or the floor. Nowhere. Not even in my toy box or anything. It took Mama a few minutes to realize what I was saying—then she exclaimed, "Ewww!"

Yes, the Intruder eats ears. How icky is that? So I've decided that if Miss Moo can't help herself and insists on being bad (Mama calls it neurotic, but that's just another word for bad), then I'm going to have to fix this myself. Grandma, I am going to eat Maggie's ears. It's just that simple. I'm going to chew those little floppers and chew them until they are just nubs. Then we will see how she likes it.

The only problem is that she squeals when I start getting a good chomp going. So I'm going to have to start chewing on her when she is asleep. That shouldn't be too hard, though, because Maggie can't tell time and I can sneak up on her when she is napping.

I know I've talked before about how I can read and add and subtract (well, some), but I wanted to tell you that I can tell time too. Mama said that clocks and watches were invented when people had to learn how to catch trains on time. Because I don't have to run to catch a train (but I could if I wanted to), I tell time in a different way. Mostly, unless dinnertime is coming, I divide time into bigger blocks. It is like this:

BMT: Benson Morning Time (a lot like treat time)
BAT: Benson Afternoon Time (a lot like BMT)
BPT: Benson Play Time (not to be confused with BPPT)
BPPT: Benson Plotting & Planning Time (takes place mostly in the Spy Wolf cave)
BBT: Benson Bed Time (I take a toy with all of its arms and legs and run up the stairs)
BTT: Benson Treat Time (in other words, *all* the time!)
BST: Benson Sleep Time (all legs up in the air)

I'm going to have to add in some new times for those special dates with Princess Sophie, maybe SDT—Sophie Date Time. She has finally agreed to come over to watch a movie with me, and we have even agreed on the movie. We are going to watch *Shrek*, Grandma, and I've asked Mama and Sam to not be in the room and stare at us so we can have a good time. Alone. Mama said she would make us some popcorn with catnip over it too (I like butter better, but I can compromise).

My only problem is that darn Moo. (I know, I said darn, but I really mean it). Maybe Mama can tell her to stay upstairs, but I know her. She will sit on the landing and stare at us. Here is what she will do right when the movie gets good: Maggie will take one of my soup bones and drop it down the steps, one at a time, and then it will clonk onto the dining room floor and just ruin the moment. She is sneaky. Maybe I can get Mama to take her out on the deck for a few hours. Then she can bark at those mean little Vietnamese rat dogs. Outside.

Anyway, Grandma and Granddad, I've got to go. Mama's birthday is coming up soon. What do you think I should get her? I was thinking about a used Piggy, but that might be too obvious as a hint that I want a new one.

CHAPTER 24

A SPY WOLF CHRISTMAS

The Spy Wolf pressed forward, gliding silently in the darkness. Not a creature was stirring, not even a mouse. As he passed the window, his silver nub tail glowed softly in the moonlight. In the next second, he moved back into the shadows, invisible again. No one knew he was inside the restricted area, moving rapidly and on a mission. It wasn't the stockings hung by the chimney with care. Benson knew there was no chimney and that the stockings, while full of red and green holiday rawhides, were hidden on the kitchen counter, far away from the swiping paws of prying Spy Wolves or even dog boys.

The Spy Wolf's nose twitched at an unfamiliar scent. It smelled like pine cleaner. Or maybe it was the tree. A tree inside! What were they thinking? Those lights were so bright. Good thing Mama turned them off when she went to bed.

The Spy Wolf took out his secret spy flashlight from his spy-kit backpack and trained it at the large array of boxes. He had to answer two important questions before returning to the Spy Cave: 1) Which ones held Christmas presents for him? 2) Were his presents bigger and did he have more than Maggie?

Maybe that was three questions, but that wasn't important. What was important was that the Spy Wolf was number one in the hearts of his many admirers and that girl dogs everywhere worshipped him. Again his nub tail wagged all by itself. Sometimes he just couldn't help it. It must have been because he thought about girls, and thinking about girls made him think about Sophie and the present he hoped she had sent for him. He had one for her: *The Dangerous Book for Cats.*

Actually, Benson didn't think the book was that dangerous, and it was incomplete anyway. He wrote inside the back cover how all cat girls could have great adventures by helping the Spy Wolf make the world safe for dog boys by sending aliens back to outer space. He could just hear her now! She would cry out, "Oh my Lion King, Benson. This is puuurfect!"

Benson came out of his daydream with a start! The Spy Wolf had to move quickly. He knew he had been inside the restricted area for too long. Soon the sentries would be making their rounds, and he didn't want to be discovered. Last year Benson had been caught opening some of his presents early, and Mama had scolded him. That memory was bad, and he licked his lips at the thought.

Then click—the light went on upstairs. Grandma, I had to run up the stairs and hop onto Mama's bed while trying to look innocent. Luckily for me, Mama was on her way into the bathroom, and she was sleepy, so she didn't see me jump down again and run for the Spy Cave. She gets worried when I play Spy Wolf in the middle of the night. I guess it's because I have to bark some and make yipping noises. Not that the Moo ever wakes up. She snores right through all of the great Spy Wolf adventures.

I asked Santa for a Wii Fit and a rope ladder this year. Sophie can use the rope ladder to climb in the window to the Spy Cave, and I can set up the Wii for games, and we can play Spy Wolf and Cat Woman.

I have decided I do like Maggie Moo. This year, she is going to wear the silly snowman costume they bought for me last year. Ha! I like that a lot. She already has my hand-me-down sweaters, and she even likes to play dress-up. She is like that silly house elf in the Harry Potter books. She is just happy she has clothes. If she only knew!

Well, Grandma, I should go to sleep now. That way I will be well rested and ready to get Mama up by 5:30 AM so we can go out. Mama calls it "O-dark-30," and she doesn't like it much, but then we come back and have a good nap. I thought you might like this picture of me in the Spy Cave. You might notice you can't see any treats in here, right? That is because all of my toys and bones are invisible when they are inside the Spy Cave. That way Maggie can't see them!

DOG BOY RECIPES

BABY FOOD COOKIES

Steak is my favorite food, and Auntie Debra has figured out a way for me to have it in a cookie. I don't usually like people baby food, but these are really really yummy. These smell really good while they are cooking in the oven, and I especially like them for breakfast. I think four or five make a great breakfast for a working dog!

Get:
4 2^1/$_2$-oz jars of Beef & Beef Broth baby food
^{1}/$_2$ cup of powdered milk
^{1}/$_2$ cup of cream of wheat cereal or textured vegetable protein (TVP)** (by itself, this would be yuk!)
^{1}/$_2$ cup of brown and wild rice medley, uncooked

Do:
Preheat the oven to 350 degrees Fahrenheit. Stir all the ingredients together until well combined.

Use a small ice cream scoop, or rounded teaspoon, to make individual cookies on a lightly greased baking sheet.

Bake for 15 minutes. Remove from the oven and let the cookies cool. Taste a half dozen or so to make sure they are okay.

Keep the treats refrigerated because they are a little bit soft and moist in the middle. They keep for up to a week in the refrigerator. This recipe makes about two dozen cookies.

** Auntie Debra uses TVP for my friends who are allergic to wheat or when I need more protein in my diet. She says TVP may also be substituted for the milk for dogs who are allergic to dairy products.

BACON & CHEDDAR CRACKERS

These cookies are crisp and great to munch on while you are watching Animal Planet or Food Network or my favorite movie, *Lady and the Tramp*.

Get:
4 cups all-purpose flour (plus more for rolling)
10 tablespoon vegetable shortening, chilled
2 cups cheddar cheese, shredded and lightly packed
6 slices bacon, cooked and finely chopped
$1^1/_2$ cups ice cold water

Do:
Preheat the oven to 400 degrees Fahrenheit. Pulse the flour and shortening in a food processor until it resembles coarse meal. Pulse again while incorporating the cheese and bacon. Slowly drizzle in the cold water until a ball forms.

Remove the dough from the bowl onto a lightly floured surface. Sprinkle the ball with more flour. Roll out the dough to the desired thickness, and cut it into desired shapes.

Place the dough on baking trays and bake 20 to 25 minutes. Remove the crackers from the oven and let them cool completely. This recipe makes about three trays of treats, but they go fast!

MUTTZA BALLS

Even though Auntie Debra says you can make these with beef, pork, turkey, or chicken, let's face it—beef is what's for dinner. And breakfast. And lunch. Snacks too. This recipe has veggies in it because Auntie Debra thinks she just *has* to sneak some into my diet. I think you should feel free to leave the veggies out and replace with more meat.

Get:
1 lb lean meat (beef, pork, turkey, or chicken)
1 cup of oatmeal (good for canine cholesterol)
$1/4$ cup of carrots, shredded
$1/4$ cup of celery, shredded
$1/4$ cup of zucchini, shredded
1 clove of garlic, minced
$1/2$ cup of parsley, finely chopped
1 teaspoon sea salt
1-2 large eggs
$1/2$ cup panko bread crumbs
$1/4$ cup flax seed, finely processed
Olive oil as needed

Do:
Preheat the oven to 350 degrees Fahrenheit. Mix all the ingredients together and form into bite-sized balls using an ice cream scoop.

Place the balls on baking sheets and bake 25 to 40 minutes until cooked through. Store covered in the refrigerator for up to five days (if they last that long). This makes about 40 balls if you don't eat too many right as they come out of the oven.

MOO STEW

Maggie Moo likes this. But then, she will eat the ears off a stuffed toy. It is actually good, even though it has vegetables in it.

Get:
1 lb chicken thighs, cubed
1 tablespoon vegetable oil
$1^1/_2$ cups of peas and carrots
1 cup green beans
$^1/_2$ cup of cooked pasta

Do:
Brown the chicken in the vegetable oil. Add the vegetables and cook until the vegetables are soft. Mix in the cooked pasta and cool to room temperature before serving. This makes about four days of Moo dinner servings.